YORK NOTES

T0351591

SPELLING, PUNCTUATION & GRAMMAR

WORKBOOK

ELIZABETH WALTER AND KATE WOODFORD

YORK PRESS
322 Old Brompton Road, London SW5 9JH

PEARSON EDUCATION LIMITED
Edinburgh Gate, Harlow,
Essex CM20 2JE, United Kingdom
Associated companies, branches and representatives throughout the world

First published 2017

23
12

ISBN 978–1–2921–8637–5

Phototypeset by DTP Media
Printed in Great Britain by Ashford Colour Press Ltd.

Photo credits: Africa Studio/Shutterstock for page 14 top / Lim Yong Hian/Shutterstock for page bottom / Alexander Zinovoy/Shutterstock for page 25 bottom / smikeymikey 1/Shutterstock for page 26 bottom / Eric Isselee/Shutterstock for page 31 bottom / Arijuhani/© iStock for 35 bottom / Rawpixel.com/Shutterstock for page 42 bottom / Lighthunter/Shutterstock for page 43 bottom / Africa Studio/Shutterstock for page 45 bottom / Khomulo Anna/Shutterstock for page 46 bottom / Iakov Filimonov/Shutterstock for page 51 bottom / Joe Dunckley/Shutterstock for page 54 bottom /

CONTENTS

PART FIVE: PARAGRAPHS AND ORGANISATION

PART SIX: PROGRESS BOOSTER

PART SEVEN: ANSWERS

HOW TO USE YOUR SPELLING, PUNCTUATION AND GRAMMAR WORKBOOK

There are many ways in which this Workbook can support your study and revision of spelling, punctuation and grammar. There is no 'right' way – choose the one that suits your learning style best.

Alongside the York Notes Study Guide	As a 'standalone' revision programme	As a form of mock-exam
Do you have the York Notes Study Guide for spelling, punctuation and grammar? The contents of this Workbook are designed to match the sections in the Study Guide, so with both books to hand you could: ● Read the relevant section(s) of the Study Guide ● Complete the tasks in the corresponding section in your Workbook	Think you know your spelling, punctuation and grammar well? Why not work through the Workbook systematically from beginning to end? You could make a revision diary and allocate particular sections of the Workbook to various slots in your week.	Prefer to do all your revision in one go? You could put aside a day or two and work through the Workbook, page by page. Once you have finished, check all your answers in one go! This will be quite a challenge, but it may be the approach you prefer.

HOW WILL THE WORKBOOK HELP YOU TEST YOUR KNOWLEDGE AND SKILLS?

Part One: This short test will help you to find out which areas of spelling, punctuation and grammar you need to work on.

Parts Two to Five: These offer a range of tasks to practise specific areas of spelling, punctuation and grammar – for example, key conjunctions in Part Three ('Get your grammar right!') and colons and semicolons in Section Four ('Punctuation for accuracy and effect'). Each section ends with a 'Test your understanding' task to consolidate your learning.

Part Six: With this written 'Progress booster' task, you can put into practice all that you have learnt about spelling, punctuation and grammar. You can then compare your written piece with graded sample responses and read an expert marker's view of the three pieces.

This is just a summary of what this book contains. There is much more here to help you brush up on your SPaG, including:

● Practice of difficult areas of punctuation that can catch you out, such as contractions and apostrophes
● Vocabulary tasks that will help to add interest and detail to your writing
● Help with words that are easily confused

SPAG CHECK

Work through these questions to find out how good you are at spelling, punctuation and grammar (or SPaG). Check your answers at the back and decide what you most need to work on.

1 Circle the correct **spelling** in each pair:

a) apparent / apparant

b) privelige / privilege

c) persistent / persistant

d) definitely / definately

e) weird / wierd

f) admitedly / admittedly

g) awfull / awful

h) parallel / paralel

i) heros / heroes

2 Write the correct **word class** of the underlined word in each sentence. Use the list of options below:

a) I suddenly <u>realised</u> who I was speaking to. ....

b) The <u>suffering</u> around her was terrible. ....

c) We called <u>her</u> immediately. ....

d) Zara was wearing the most <u>amazing</u> dress. ....

e) She spoke so <u>quickly</u>. ....

f) I found the letter <u>in</u> a drawer. ....

g) He called <u>while</u> you were sleeping. ....

h) I'm happy to meet in <u>either</u> café. ....

preposition	determiner	pronoun	conjunction
adjective	noun	verb	adverb

3 Are these **concrete nouns** (C), **abstract nouns** (A) or **proper nouns** (P)? Tick the correct box.

a) ambition   C ☐   A ☐   P ☐

b) forehead   C ☐   A ☐   P ☐

c) window   C ☐   A ☐   P ☐

d) Jupiter   C ☐   A ☐   P ☐

e) concentration   C ☐   A ☐   P ☐

f) Sahara   C ☐   A ☐   P ☐

g) tablet   C ☐   A ☐   P ☐

4 Are the underlined **past participles** of the verbs in these sentences correct (✓) or incorrect (✗)? If incorrect, provide the correct form.

a) He insisted that he hadn't <u>broke</u> the law.   ❏ ....

b) As a child, she had <u>showed</u> so much promise as a dancer.   ❏ ....

c) Her little boy had <u>drew</u> her a picture.   ❏ ....

d) Carlo is fed up because his team got <u>beat</u>.   ❏ ....

e) I'd <u>bet</u> Daniel that he couldn't swim twenty lengths without stopping.   ❏ ....

f) Anika had climbed the tree and <u>shook</u> the branches.   ❏ ....

g) By the time I arrived, Sanjay had already <u>drank</u> his coffee.   ❏ ....

h) The room was hot and she'd <u>began</u> to feel slightly faint.   ❏ ....

5 Add **commas** in the correct place in these sentences:

a) Even though she has plenty of money she still complains.

b) My sister who never takes any exercise still managed to run faster than me!

c) She handed him a small black box.

d) Could you come here Otis?

e) Similarly temperatures may vary quite considerably.

f) You've been to Mexico haven't you?

g) Madrid which is the capital of Spain is in the middle of the country.

h) It's hot in here isn't it?

6 Is the use of **apostrophes** in these sentences correct (✓) or incorrect (✗)? If incorrect, provide the correct form.

a) The dog ran after it's ball.   ❏ ....

b) She fought for womens' equality.   ❏ ....

c) Those two at the back are the childrens' bedrooms.   ❏ ....

d) Naomi and I often wear each other's clothes.   ❏ ....

e) You need a lot of tomatoes' for the recipe.   ❏ ....

f) My grandfather was born in the '40s.   ❏ ....

g) The last slice of cake is your's.   ❏ ....

h) Our aunt and uncle's house is in the countryside.   ❏ ....

TEST YOUR UNDERSTANDING

Correct any spelling, punctuation and grammar errors that you can find in this extract from a student's essay and then rewrite it in the space below. There are **ten** erros in total. Check your answers on page 57 and decide which areas you need to practise.

Errors to look out for in the writing include:

● Words that are spelt incorrectly

● Words that have been confused with other words that sound the same

● Missing punctuation

As he steps out on to the street, he feels a heat that is more intense then anything he can remember. He has never been more hot. Its oppressive and unrelenting, and all but takes his breath away. He makes his way, slowly, to the market square. The square is seething with people, eager to catch a glimpse of the dancers. Intrigued, he joins them, weaving his way in. As if from nowhere, a blizzard of crimson petals and torn fragments of paper suddenly decends, turning the air momentarily pink, it comes slowly to rest on the heads and shoulders of the eager onlookers. A young girl next to him, her eyes round with wonder, dissapears into the crowd as if sucked in by an irresistible force. Somewhere beyond the wall of bodies, someone beats out a rythm on the drums, sending a ripple of excitement through the crowd. He strains every nerve to see passed the wall of people in front of him, but to no avail. There are just to many bodies. He gives in to the will of the crowd and lets himself be buffeted one way and then another. He looks up. Above him, the sky is a watercolour painting of pink red and orange.

COMMON SPELLING ERRORS

Words can be difficult to spell for a variety of reasons. In some words, the **vowels** (a, e, i, o and u) are unpredictable, while in other words it is hard to remember whether the **consonants** are single or double. For this reason, it is important to learn difficult spellings.

1 Fill the gaps in these words with the correct **vowels**:

　　a) The car wasn't even moving – it was station ... ry.

　　b) For no appar ... nt reason, Sophia suddenly stopped in her tracks and grabbed my hand.

　　c) So do you think it's become more socially accept ... ble to use a phone at the dinner table?

　　d) He's such an amazing guy – it was a real priv ... l ... ge to meet him.

　　e) The physics and chemistry departments are in sep ... r ... te buildings.

　　f) Santiago's team will defin ... t ... ly win the match tomorrow.

2 Circle the spelling in each of these sentences that has the correct number of **consonants**:

　　a) You can bring some money if you like, but it won't be [necessary / neccessary].

　　b) I had lasagne for my main course and chocolate cake for [dessert / desert].

　　c) Do you have her email [adress / address]?

　　d) I found myself in a [dilemma / dilema] and really didn't know what to do.

　　e) [Admitedly / Admittedly], I hadn't handled the situation very well.

　　f) He later became a [successful / sucessful] inventor.

3 Write the correct **spelling** of the misspelt words in these sentences. (There are one or two misspelt words in each sentence.)

　　a) Her face looked vaguely familair, but I couldn't put a name to her.

　　　..

　　b) They say that if you have a really persistant cough, you should see a doctor.

　　　..

　　c) I don't know why Fabio even raised the issue. It wasn't relevent to the discussion.

　　　..

　　d) There was very little accomodation available becuase we'd left it so late to arrange.

　　　..

　　e) There are parralels between the two situations but they're not completely analagous.

　　　..

　　f) Luisa was embarassed when she forgot the words to the song, but no one noticed.

　　　..

PART TWO: SPELLINGS FOR SUCCESS

4 Tick the correct **spelling** in each pair of words:

a) argument	☐	arguement	☐
b) guage	☐	gauge	☐
c) completely	☐	completly	☐
d) liason	☐	liaison	☐
e) accidently	☐	accidentally	☐
f) noticeable	☐	noticable	☐

5 Is the **spelling** of the underlined words in these sentences correct (✓) or incorrect (✗)? If incorrect, provide the correct spelling.

a) She's buried in Lake View <u>cemetary</u>, next to her son. ☐

....

b) These two products are <u>basically</u> the same. ☐

....

c) I bumped into some <u>collegues</u> of mine at the gig. ☐

....

d) I'm <u>definately</u> going to take a year out to travel before university. ☐

....

e) He has <u>publically</u> apologised for the comments. ☐

....

6 Proofread this extract from a student's descriptive essay to find **six** spelling errors. Write the words with the correct spellings below.

I'd spied the woman several times in the town centre. On the first occassion, she was seated at a table for one in a small, independant café behind the public library. At first glance, her appearence seemed somewhat bizzare. She was wearing what appeared to be a large, ill-fitting coat, which stuck out at the front. It aroused my curiousity. On closer inspection, the front portion of the coat turned out to be a small dog, tucked cosily into the garment, its bony little head all that was visible. I regarded the woman and the many bags that lay at her feet, then too late became concious that she had seen me looking. Quickly, I withdrew my gaze.

a) ....

b) ....

c) ....

d) ....

e) ....

f) ....

SPELLING STRATEGIES

WORDS INSIDE WORDS

Sometimes, the difficult part of a word is itself a short word. Look out for **short words** within longer words and use this to help you remember how the longer word is spelt.

1 Fill in the gaps in these words using **short words** from the box. Note that there are two short words that you will not need. The first one has been done for you.

a) I keep having these really <u>we</u>ird dreams in which no one speaks to me.

b) Throughout the whole of this period, there was a very rigid social hier … … … … y.

c) At lunchtime, the restaurant is full of bu … … … ess people in smart suits.

d) Aged twelve, Ali was already very indepen … … … … and was cooking his own meals.

e) It is imperative that these measures are put in place to protect the env … … … … ment.

f) She's very sociable and makes fri … … … s fairly easily.

~~we~~	art	dent	cart
sin	end	arch	iron

2 Correct these **spellings**. In the correct spelling, underline the **short word** that can help you remember the difficult part of the longer word. The first one has been done for you.

a) unfortunatly …… un<u>fortun</u>ately ……

b) knowlege ………………………………

c) tendancy ………………………………

d) futher ………………………………

e) acceptible ………………………………

SYLLABLES

Long words can be especially difficult to spell. When writing a long word, it is sometimes helpful to say aloud each **syllable** of the word separately.

3 Circle the correct spelling after saying aloud each **syllable** of the word:

a) calendar / calender

b) mystery / mystry

c) categery / category

d) reference / refrence

e) contraversy / controversy

USEFUL WORDS FOR ENGLISH ESSAYS

You will find that there are certain words that you want to use frequently when writing English essays. It is worth making an effort to memorise the spellings of these words.

1 For each pair of words, tick the one that is spelt correctly:

a) character	☐	caracter	☐
b) rythm	☐	rhythm	☐
c) sylable	☐	syllable	☐
d) euphemism	☐	euphamism	☐
e) parallel	☐	paralel	☐
f) nontheless	☐	nonetheless	☐

2 Put the letters in brackets in the correct order to complete these words:

a) rep … … … tion   [iet]

b) den … … … ment   [eou]

c) onomatop … … … c   [ioe]

d) omni … … … … … nt   [csei]

e) contemp … … … … … y   [roar]

f) prot … … … nist   [gao]

3 Proofread this extract from a student's essay to find **five** spelling errors. Write the words with the correct spellings below.

> Many people who are oposed to the compulsory wearing of uniform in schools claim that uniform stifles the child's individuality. They beleive that a child's freedom to choose what to put on in the morning is paramount, diminishing all other considerations. I mantain that the benefits of non-uniform are overstated when compared with the advantages of uniform to the child, the child's family and the institution itself.
>
> Firstly, there is the matter of cost. Admitedly, uniform requires an initial outlay, which is undoutedly challenging for some hard-pressed parents. However, most items of uniform can now be purchased quite cheaply from high-street supermarkets.

a) ....

b) ....

c) ....

d) ....

e) ....

LETTER ORDER, SILENT LETTERS AND PLURALS

It is worth spending some time learning the rules of English spelling – and the exceptions to these rules.

THE 'I BEFORE E EXCEPT...' RULE

1 Fill the gaps in these words with 'ie' or 'ei':

a) She had ach ... ... ved all her goals.

b) Pranav had rec ... ... ved the message and ignored it.

c) At this time, for ... ... gn travel was a luxury for most people.

d) Roughly ten per cent of the Earth is covered by glac ... ... rs.

e) To be polite, she f ... ... gned interest in the subject.

f) Without warning, Alice s ... ... zed the object and threw it out of the window.

SILENT LETTERS

2 Add a **silent letter** from the box below to one word in each of these sentences:

a) Sadly, my nowledge of the subject is limited.

....

b) She wispered gently in his ear.

....

c) Above her, leaves rusled in the breeze.

....

d) Queen Victoria reined for over sixty-three years.

....

e) Later that night, someone nocked on the door.

....

f) She campained tirelessly for women's rights.

....

h	t	g	g	k	k

3 Is the **spelling** of the underlined words in these sentences correct (✓) or incorrect (✗)? If incorrect, provide the correct spelling.

a) The city was badly <u>bommed</u> in the war. ☐ ....

b) The two words <u>ryme</u>. ☐ ....

c) I was suddenly <u>conscious</u> of everyone staring at me. ☐ ....

d) Antonio <u>fassened</u> his coat and walked on. ☐ ....

DIFFICULT PLURALS

4 Write the correct **plural form** of these words:

a) dress   ....

b) hero   ....

c) half   ....

d) belief   ....

e) criterion   ....

f) series   ....

g) quiz   ....

h) echo   ....

5 Tick the correct **plural form** in each pair of words:

a) tomatoes	☐	tomatos	☐
b) countrys	☐	countries	☐
c) roofs	☐	rooves	☐
d) knives	☐	knifes	☐
e) discoes	☐	discos	☐
f) deer	☐	deers	☐
g) runner-ups	☐	runners-up	☐
h) volcanos	☐	volcanoes	☐

6 Proofread this extract from a student's piece of descriptive writing to find the **four** incorrectly spelt plural forms. Write the words with the correct spellings below.

> Alone in the forest, I lay down on a bed of leafs and gazed up through the trees' dense network of limbs and twigs. With nothing to distract me, my senses became strangely heightened and I was suddenly aware of all the life around me, from the flys that buzzed around my head to the myriad of birds perched in the branchs above. Nothing seemed quite still – everything vibrated with life. I closed my eyes and listened to the echoes of a million lifes that had been lived before.

a) ....

b) ....

c) ....

d) ....

COMMONLY CONFUSED WORDS

There are several words in English that sound the same but that have quite different spellings and meanings.

1 Choose a word from each pair in the box to complete these sentences:

a) How does his medical condition .... his health generally?

b) There's a band playing every night .... Tuesdays.

c) I can't .... the smell of cheese when it's cooking.

d) The driver had to .... sharply to avoid hitting her.

e) Try not to .... your phone this time, Luca!

f) The magician created the .... that he was floating.

g) I was nervous, so Natalia advised me to sit down and .... deeply.

brake/break	*bear/bare*	*lose/loose*	*affect/effect*
accept/except	*allusion/illusion*	*breathe/breath*	

2 Circle the correct word in these sentences:

a) I'm a bit tired – I think I'm going to take a [brake / break].

b) It's far too cold for [bare / bear] legs!

c) You've lost so much weight! Look how [loose / lose] your trousers are!

d) I walk [past / passed] his office on the way to work.

e) He's certainly a better dancer [than / then] his brother!

f) I was pleased when my teacher [complimented / complemented] my work.

g) We were so full! We couldn't possibly have eaten [dessert / desert].

3 Is the underlined word in each sentence correct (✓) or incorrect (✗)? If incorrect, write the correct word.

a) I'm not going to the nine o'clock lecture. It's <u>to</u> early for me. ☐ ....

b) Time <u>past</u> far too quickly and it was soon time to say goodbye. ☐ ....

c) Accommodation here is much cheaper <u>then</u> it is in London. ☐ ....

d) 'I love exploring new cities.' 'Me <u>too</u>.' ☐ ....

e) I just hope she doesn't <u>brake</u> his heart! ☐ ....

f) Veronika <u>led</u> her team to victory in the championship. ☐ ....

g) That was really rude. He shouldn't <u>of</u> said that. ☐ ....

PREFIXES AND SUFFIXES

Prefixes and **suffixes** are small groups of letters that are added to words to change their meaning.

1 Match the **prefixes** to their meanings:

a) un-	not
b) mis-	wrongly or badly
c) re-	too much
d) pre-	again
e) dis-	before
f) over-	opposite to

2 Circle the correct **spelling**:

a) dissimilar / disimilar

b) boredom / bordom

c) awfull / awful

d) mishapen / misshapen

e) stoping / stopping

f) becoming / becomeing

g) uglyness / ugliness

3 Fill the gaps in these words with the correct **prefixes** and **suffixes**. The number of letters varies.

a) I'm afraid I .... spelt his name. I wrote two ts instead of one.

b) Both children were gap................... at me in disbelief.

c) They were .... satisfied with the service and decided to complain.

d) It was nice to see Daniela. We chat................... over a cup of coffee.

e) Is she cop................... okay with her new responsibilities?

f) It was so .... fair that we got extra homework.

g) Hari was grate................... for all the presents he received for his birthday.

4 Proofread this extract from a student's essay to find **four** incorrectly spelt words. Write the words with the correct spellings below.

> The dog wouldn't leave her alone. He would paw at her leg, or cock his head to one side, fixing her with a reproachfull stare, hopeing for just one scrap of affection. She found his attentivness touching, but it made her feel guilty. She pated him on the head and looked away.

a) ....

b) ....

c) ....

d) ....

TEST YOUR UNDERSTANDING

Read this extract from a student's piece of narrative writing to find **ten** spelling errors. Rewrite the extract with the words spelt correctly in the space below.

Look out for the following types of spelling mistakes:

- Words with the incorrect number of consonants or vowels in the wrong order
- Incorrect plural nouns
- Words that have been confused with other words that sound the same

Sylvie sidled passed a cluster of people and made for the exit. No one was looking. She fassened her coat and slipped out of the church through it's hefty wooden door. Checking first that it was deserted, she headed to the churchyard. The snow and old leafs had been brushed from the paving stones and what now remained underfoot was a slick of ice that made walking almost impossible. She made her way gingerly, steadying herself against the wall of the church with one bear hand till her fingers were num with cold. The ancient yew tree that crouched over the gravestones was laden with snow. Its branchs hung low with the sheer wieght of frozen water. Suddenly smitten by the snow's eerie beauty in the dim light, Sylvie stopped to gaze around her. Yesterday's weather forcast had promised overnight snow and when she woke this morning, her whole room was suffused by a pinkish light, Sylvie had not been dissapointed.

VOCABULARY FOR IMPACT

It is important to use a wide range of **vocabulary**, especially in creative and descriptive writing. This can add detail and interest to your writing, and help you avoid repetition.

1 Find three **synonyms** in the box below for each word:

a) reduce   ....

b) grip   ....

c) spare   ....

d) graceful   ....

e) fast   ....

f) appropriate ....

clutch	supple	suitable	swift	grasp
surplus	diminish	rapid	lithe	excess
apt	fitting	shrink	cling	superfluous
nimble	dwindle	brisk		

2 Circle the **strongest** or **most powerful** word from the options given in each sentence. The first one has been done for you.

a) The children were living in [dirty / squalid / unhygienic] conditions.

b) The man led us into a [vast / very large / spacious] hall.

c) Closing the factory was a [daft / foolish / ludicrous] decision.

d) We were all [alarmed / petrified / fearful] when we heard the gunfire.

e) The team's [careful / thorough / meticulous] preparation paid off.

f) She was [upset / devastated / miserable] when her jewellery was stolen.

3 In each group, circle the option that has the most **negative connotation**. The first one has been done for you.

a) exclusive / elitist / expensive / lavish

b) fawn over / admire / compliment / flatter

c) vibrant / vivid / garish / colourful

d) cherish / safeguard / protect / mollycoddle

e) chivalrous / courteous / smarmy / gallant

f) funny / hilarious / laughable / amusing

WHAT ARE WORD CLASSES?

The term **word class** (sometimes called part of speech) refers to a type of word – for example, **noun**, **verb**, **adjective** or **pronoun**.

1 Write the words listed below in the correct rows of the table. Remember that some words might belong to more than one **word class**.

Nouns	
Pronouns	
Verbs	
Prepositions	
Adjectives	
Adverbs	
Conjunctions	
Determiners	

quietly	underneath	my	and	it
walk	the	but	ridiculous	hardly
describe	over	them	fast	contentment
serious	on	pride	who	export
portray	or	each	however	from

2 Underline the words that should begin with a capital letter because they are **proper nouns**:

a) The play was first performed in the soviet union in 1946 and is one of priestley's best-known works.

b) The actor john gielgud staged a version of *romeo and juliet* using elizabethan costumes.

c) Mr jones is the original owner of manor farm, where *animal farm* is set.

d) Papa is daljit's husband and he comes from lahore in what is now pakistan.

3 Tick the boxes to indicate which nouns are **abstract** and which are **concrete**, which are **countable** and which **uncountable**:

	Abstract	Concrete	Countable	Uncountable
a) ocean	☐	☐	☐	☐
b) socialism	☐	☐	☐	☐
c) police officer	☐	☐	☐	☐
d) warmth	☐	☐	☐	☐

PRONOUNS AND DETERMINERS

Pronouns are words such as 'she', 'it' and 'they'. **Possessive pronouns** are words such as 'my', 'our' and 'theirs'. They are used to replace nouns or noun phrases, usually in order to avoid repetition. **Determiners** are words such as 'a', 'the' and 'every'. They are used directly before nouns. Determiners have various functions, including indicating number, amount and ownership.

4 Circle the correct **pronouns** and **determiners** in these sentences:

    a) You'll need a coat if [your / you're] going out.

    b) Hatice and [I / me] are going to the cinema.

    c) You should see [they're / their] house – [it's / its enormous]!

    d) Do you know [who's / whose] jacket this is?

    e) [Your / You're] dog is walking as though [it's / its] leg hurts.

    f) Have you seen [mine / my] bag?

    g) [They're / There] going to be late because of the traffic.

ADJECTIVES AND ADVERBS

Adjectives are words such as 'blue', 'descriptive' and 'figurative'. They are used to add description and detail to writing. Adverbs have several functions, including describing how an action is done, for example, 'quietly', 'badly'.

5 Change these **adjectives** into **adverbs**:

    a) quick   ....

    b) easy   ....

    c) reluctant   ....

    d) good   ....

    e) polite   ....

    f) doubtful   ....

    g) active   ....

6 Use the **adjectives** or **adverbs** from Task 5 to complete these sentences:

    a) I shook the headteacher's hand .... as we were introduced.

    b) Lena looked at me .... when I suggested a swim in the cold sea.

    c) I was .... to travel with Riko because I didn't like her much.

    d) We had to run .... to get there before closing time.

    e) I really hope that Goran does .... in his exams.

    f) She's so wealthy, she could .... afford to take a taxi.

    g) It is important to lead an .... lifestyle.

CLAUSES AND TYPES OF SENTENCES

CLAUSES

Clauses are short sentences or parts of longer, more complex sentences. Every clause has a subject and a verb. A **main clause** makes sense on its own, but a **subordinate clause** needs the main clause with it in order to make sense.

Subject   Verb

Scrooge repents eventually, even though it takes a profound change in personality.

Main clause   Subordinate clause

1 Underline the **subject** and the **verb** in each of these clauses:

    a) Our teacher gave us too much homework.

    b) The car started straight away.

    c) The book on the table is about African animals.

    d) Why don't you give the money to Jan?

    e) All of Maria's children enjoy playing tennis.

2 How many **clauses** are there in each sentence? Write the number.

    a) Although she is nine in the story, Anita narrates it from the perspective of her adult self. [   ]

    b) Romeo kills himself because he thinks that Juliet is dead and he is grief-stricken.   [   ]

    c) *An Inspector Calls* is one of the classics of mid-twentieth century English theatre.   [   ]

    d) The poet uses imagery connected with winter and with flight.   [   ]

    e) While Duncan is asleep, Macbeth stabs him.   [   ]

3 Is the underlined part of these sentences a **main clause** (M) or a **subordinate clause** (S)? Write the letter.

    a) Scrooge learns that unless the course of events changes, <u>Tiny Tim will die</u>.   [   ]

    b) Tiny Tim is a happy child, <u>even though he is ill</u>.   [   ]

    c) <u>Utterson is instinctively repulsed by Hyde</u> although he has no physical defects.   [   ]

    d) Lanyon tells Utterson to open the letter <u>only if Jekyll dies or disappears</u>.   [   ]

    e) If the fire hadn't gone out, <u>the boys might have been rescued</u>.   [   ]

    f) <u>While the boys sleep</u>, Captain Benson escapes into the jungle.   [   ]

TYPES OF SENTENCES

Different types of sentence are used for different effects. They can vary the pace of a piece of writing and help to hold the reader's interest.

4 Match each **sentence type** in the box below with the correct definition.

a) a short sentence that does not have a main clause

....

b) a sentence with two or more main clauses

....

c) a sentence with only one clause

....

d) a sentence with two or more clauses, at least one of which is a subordinate clause

....

simple sentence	*compound sentence*	*complex sentence*	*minor sentence*

5 Look at this extract from a student's response to a creative writing task. Write the sentence numbers next to the **sentence types**.

> **[1]** Disaster! **[2]** The tide had come in and was lapping against the foot of the cliff. **[3]** Pete and Arjun looked at one another in horror. **[4]** There was no sign of Vihaan anywhere. **[5]** He must have gone back up to the clifftop while they were in the cave. **[6]** Pete and Arjun knew they had to get away quickly, but there was no route back along the beach. **[7]** There was only one way out of there. **[8]** Upwards.

a) simple sentence ....

b) compound sentence ....

c) complex sentence ....

d) minor sentence ....

6 Rewrite these sentences so the words are in the correct order. Then, identify each sentence as simple (S), compound (C), complex (X) or minor (M).

a) she was / saw the / amazed / palace, / when Reeva

.... [   ]

b) said / least / mended / soonest

.... [   ]

c) her birthday / Mira / vase for / a beautiful glass / Lukas gave

.... [   ]

d) reading / relax, / helps me / whereas yoga / doesn't

.... [   ]

CONJUNCTIONS

Conjunctions are words that link clauses in sentences. **Coordinating conjunctions** such as 'and', 'but' and 'or' link two main clauses. **Subordinating conjunctions** such as 'while', 'although' and 'if' link a main clause and a subordinate clause.

7 Choose a **conjunction** from the box below to complete each sentence. There is one conjunction that you will not need.

a) .... Goole calls himself an inspector, he is not a member of the local police force.

b) Sheila is glad that Gerald has told the truth .... she still takes off her engagement ring.

c) .... Elizabeth learns that Lydia has run away with Wickham, she tells Darcy the news.

d) Lady Catherine insists that Elizabeth should not marry Darcy .... she wants him to marry her own daughter.

e) Mrs Bennet says she will never see Elizabeth again .... she marries Mr Collins.

f) Prospero thinks that .... Ferdinand and Miranda fall in love too easily, their love may not last.

g) Prospero realises that his disloyal brother is on a nearby ship .... he causes a tempest.

although	or	so	since
unless	but	when	if

8 Reverse the **order of clauses** in these sentences, if it is possible to do so. The first one has been done for you.

a) Although Meena's mother sometimes has bad moods, she appears calm to the outside world.
   Meena's mother appears calm to the outside world although she sometimes has bad moods.

b) Meena tells lies because she does not want to get into trouble.

   ....

c) The aunties criticise Meena but also shower her with affection.

   ....

d) Unless they get rid of the farmer, the animals cannot control the farm.

   ....

e) Major dies, so Snowball and Napoleon become the leaders.

   ....

f) Snowball orders the animals to retreat when the farmers launch an attack.

   ....

USING SENTENCES ACCURATELY

COMMON ERRORS

It is important to use sentences accurately. Avoid **run-on sentences** and **comma splices** by checking that any sentence with two main clauses either has a coordinating conjunction or is divided into separate sentences. Do not accidentally create **sentence fragments** by missing a necessary part such as a subject or verb, or begin a sentence with a **coordinating conjunction** in formal writing.

1 Which of these sentences or sentence pairs are **accurate** and **suitable for formal writing**? Correct the ones with errors. There may be more than one possible way to correct the errors.

    a) The opening paragraph is extremely dramatic, it grabs the reader's interest.

    ....

    b) In this poem, the colour yellow is often associated with decay. And red is associated with danger.

    ....

    c) Even though the narrator seems honest, we understand that what he tells us is not a true interpretation of events.

    ....

    d) I was not able to join my friends at the cinema. Too much work to do.

    ....

    e) The vocabulary in this poem is very simple, making the message even more powerful.

    ....

2 Write a suitable **conjunction** in the second sentence of each pair to correct the **comma splice** errors in the first sentence:

    a) I was instinctively afraid of the man, that's why I hid in the cupboard when I heard him approach.

    I was instinctively afraid of the man .... I hid in the cupboard when I heard him approach.

    b) I looked everywhere for the ring, I didn't find it.

    I looked everywhere for the ring .... I didn't find it.

    c) We couldn't read the letter, it was too dark.

    We couldn't read the letter .... it was too dark.

    d) We could have pizza, alternatively we could go for a burger and chips.

    We could have pizza .... we could go for a burger and chips.

SUBJECT AND VERB AGREEMENT

In a grammatically correct sentence, the form of the verb always matches the subject of the clause.

3 Write a suitable **auxiliary verb** to complete each sentence. The first one has been done for you.

a) The novel .... *was* .... written just after the end of the First World War.

b) Neither character .... portrayed in a sympathetic light.

c) The boy believes that everyone else .... seen the letter already.

d) There is a lot that Harri .... understand about life in London yet.

e) By this point in the novel, Kathy, together with her friends Ruth and Tommy, ... moved to a residential complex.

f) The characters .... all given names that reflect their personalities.

4 Circle the correct **verb form** in each sentence. If both forms are possible, circle them both.

a) I met with some of my friends from college and they [was / were] all talking about the gig.

b) Her family [want / wants] to move away from the village.

c) Alliteration occurs in several places in the poem and [emphasises / emphasise] its rhythmic quality.

d) Neither Harri's father nor his baby sister [is / are] with him in London.

e) Apart from Jane and Elizabeth, all the members of the Bennet family [behave / behaves] badly.

5 Decide whether the **subject and verb agreement** is correct in these sentences. Tick the sentences where it is correct. Cross out any incorrect verbs and write the correct form on the line. The first one has been done for you.

a) His father ~~were~~ both a businessman and a local politician.   .... *was* ....

b) I have six cousins, none of whom lives in this country.   ....

c) There is three very good reasons why corporal punishment is wrong.   ....

d) Lucas visits the doctors to whom he owe his life.   ....

e) Together with her friends, Fatima has achieved a remarkable feat.   ....

f) Neither sister realises that Mr Wickham is lying.   ....

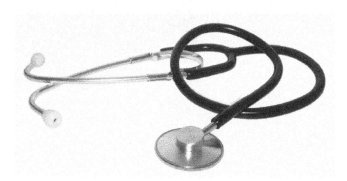

TENSES AND MODAL VERBS

USING TENSES CORRECTLY

Tense is the way verbs are used to show the time (past, present or future). It is important to use tenses accurately and to know the different forms of irregular verbs.

1 Choose a suitable **phrase** from the box below to complete these sentences:

a) I suspected that Wei and Hong .... before.

b) Scott .... some clients later today.

c) Ivan and his wife .... when they were both working in Moscow.

d) Sofia .... a lot of people in her job.

e) I'm not sure if Priya .... Nishi before.

met	meets	has met	had met	is meeting

2 Write the **past simple** and **past participle** of each of these verbs. The first one has been done for you.

a) forget   _forgot_   _forgotten_

b) build   ....

c) hide   ....

d) shrink   ....

e) steal   ....

f) pay   ....

g) think   ....

h) tear   ....

3 Use the correct **tense** of the verb in brackets to complete these sentences:

a) Omar was walking along the road when he .... something strange. (see)

b) Rosa always .... to help people if she can. (try)

c) By the time the police arrived, the robbers

.... (escape)

d) I .... with you to the hospital tomorrow if you like. (come)

e) There's a lot of work to do, and you're not leaving

until you .... it! (do)

USING MODAL VERBS

The **modal verbs** are 'can', 'could', 'may', 'might', 'shall', 'will', 'would', 'must' and 'ought'. They are used with other verbs to express basic ideas such as probability, permission, ability, advice and obligation.

4 Match the underlined **modal verb** in each sentence to its **function**. The first one has been done for you.

a) People <u>will</u> try to colonise other planets.　　　　　expressing an opinion

b) Zoe <u>must</u> have been angry.　　　　　　　　　　　expressing certainty about the future

c) Katya <u>can</u> ski pretty well.　　　　　　　　　　　expressing possibility

d) Sea levels <u>could</u> start to rise.　　　　　　　　　giving advice

e) You <u>should</u> try shopping online.　　　　　　　　expressing certainty about the past

f) The government <u>ought</u> to build more hospitals.　　expressing ability

5 Write the **full negative form** of each modal verb. The first one has been done for you.

a) can　　　　*cannot*

b) could

c) must

d) shall

e) would

f) might

g) ought to

h) will

6 Use **short forms of negative modals** to complete these sentences. Sometimes more than one answer is possible. The first one has been done for you.

a) I was upset with Martina because she ...*wouldn't*... let me borrow her car.

b) I know Marc was rude, but you .... let him upset you so much.

c) Gary says we .... disturb him because he's working on something important.

d) I only posted the parcel this afternoon, so it .... arrive tomorrow, but let me know if it does.

e) Elena .... be playing in the championship this year because she's injured.

f) The mountains are dangerous. You .... have gone there.

g) We looked for the ring all afternoon but we .... find it.

TEST YOUR UNDERSTANDING

Read this extract from a student's essay about the character of Mrs Birling in J. B. Priestley's play *An Inspector Calls.* Rewrite the extract below, correcting any grammar and spelling mistakes you find.

J. B. Priestley presents Sybil Birling as a very cold woman this is because she thinks she is better than other people. She is outraged to be under suspicion, and particularly upset that the Inspector has interrupted there party.

In Act Two she tries to bully Sheila, telling her to go to bed. Then she started to tell Inspector Goole off. She tells him that Mr Birling were a mayor and a magistrate, saying, 'You know of course that my husband was Lord Mayor only two years ago'. But the Inspector takes no notice.

Sybil Birling is a heartless person. She does not want to help the most poorest people if she thinks they haven't earnt it. For example, she tells the Inspector they've been 'helping deserving cases', this means she don't want to help people who, in her opinion, do not deserve it. In those days people had to rely of charities because there wasn't any benefits from the government.

....

....

....

....

....

....

....

....

....

....

....

....

....

....

FULL STOPS, QUESTION MARKS AND EXCLAMATION MARKS

Punctuation gives writing structure and helps the reader navigate a text. **Full stops** are used to end sentences and sometimes for initials before names and for short forms of words. **Question marks** are used at the end of a question, and **exclamation marks** indicate shock, surprise or urgency.

1 Add one of the sentences in the box below to each of these sentences, adding appropriate **punctuation** to each sentence. The first one has been done for you.

a) Karim won a million pounds in the lottery. ...... *What's he going to do with it?* ......

b) Emma wants to know if dinner's ready. ....

c) What do you think of the painting? ....

d) Would you ever go skydiving? ....

e) What did Sam say to you? ....

f) Stay away from the edge of the cliff. ....

It's beautiful, isn't it	*He asked if I was going to the movie*
Tell her it will be five minutes	*~~What's he going to do with it~~*
Not in a million years	*Don't you know how dangerous it is*

2 Add a **full stop** to these sentences in all the places where one could go:

a) His appointment with Dr Millar was scheduled for 9 am on Monday.

b) Send it back to the firm you bought it from, ie Camburst Ltd in Liverpool.

c) Some of my favourite authors, eg AA Milne and CS Lewis, wrote for children.

d) A lot of writers, artists etc live in this street, and his home is No 7.

e) Prof J Cramer and Dr V González both work at the university.

f) The Skills Corp headquarters are located at 53 Acacia Ave, Newtown.

3 Add a **question mark** or a **full stop** to the end of these sentences:

a) Georgi asked me if I wanted a glass of water

b) I wasn't sure whether she had enjoyed the party

c) Do you agree that pupils should wear a school uniform

d) Nadia's late. What could have happened to her

e) I asked if you could come to the station with me

f) Max has a lot of good ideas, don't you think

4 Tick the correct **punctuation** options. More than one option may be correct.

a) I can't believe Riko is only sixteen! ☐

I can't believe Riko is only sixteen. ☐

I can't believe Riko is only sixteen? ☐

b) Why do you think Raj wants to become a pilot! ☐

Why do you think Raj wants to become a pilot. ☐

Why do you think Raj wants to become a pilot? ☐

c) Kristyna's brother was born three years later! ☐

Kristyna's brother was born three years later. ☐

Kristyna's brother was born three years later? ☐

d) The waves were as high as a house! ☐

The waves were as high as a house. ☐

The waves were as high as a house? ☐

e) How many times have you been to Delhi! ☐

How many times have you been to Delhi. ☐

How many times have you been to Delhi? ☐

5 Rewrite the paragraph below. Divide it into five sentences. Add **capital letters, full stops, question marks** and **exclamations marks** so that it works as a piece of creative writing.

it felt as though the whole world was shaking I had never experienced anything like it whatever was happening I looked down and thought I might faint with fear the rock I was standing on was splitting in half

....

....

....

....

....

....

....

....

....

....

COMMAS

Commas are used between clauses in a sentence or to separate items in lists. When you read aloud, a comma indicates a small pause.

1 Are the **commas** used correctly or does the sentence contain a **comma splice**? Mark each sentence with ✓ or ✗. Rewrite the corrected sentences on the line below.

a) Although it was dark, I could still make out the shape of the statue. ☐

....

b) Sheena started to walk more quickly, she didn't want to be late again. ☐

....

c) I blushed to the roots of my hair, everyone was staring at me. ☐

....

d) Their house was in a small village, close to a river. ☐

....

e) The jacket was made of red velvet, it had gold buttons. ☐

....

2 Draw a line to match a clause on the left with one on the right. Add a **comma** at the end of the first clause if it is needed. Not every sentence needs a comma.

a) If the door is locked	end up being the most rewarding.
b) The plane was unable to take off	Kerry still came for a pizza with us.
c) Often, the things we find most difficult	get a key from the caretaker.
d) Whenever I go to Istanbul	because there was ice on the runway.
e) We were never allowed in my father's office	I bring back some Turkish sweets.
f) Despite having eaten earlier	when he was working.

3 Add a **comma** to these sentences in all the places where one is needed:

a) 'Good morning Donna. It's a lovely day isn't it?'

b) Although it was morning a layer of thick dark cloud still blocked the Sun.

c) We were lucky enough to spot elephants giraffes and lions which were resting under a tree.

d) Despite our best efforts the room was far from cosy.

e) 'If you want to swim make sure you bring a swimming costume a towel and plenty of sun cream won't you?'

4 Use the phrases in the box to complete these sentences. Add **commas** where they are needed.

a) Mrs Evans .... had great difficulty climbing the fence.

b) Most of the hotels .... cater for the luxury market.

c) Many of the people .... had travelled from abroad to be there.

d) The castle .... looked smaller than Chuck had expected.

in the town	*which stood at the mouth of the river*
who suffered from arthritis	*who were at the conference*

5 Rewrite these sentences, correcting the **commas**. You may need to add or delete commas, or use them to replace other punctuation.

a) Leave the area immediately, if you hear three short sharp blasts of the horn.

....

b) My friend who is very generous, bought a card; flowers and chocolates for my birthday.

....

c) The ancient, stone pots contained coins bracelets and rings.

....

d) In addition students can take part in archery, and rock climbing.

....

6 Read this extract from a student's piece of creative writing. Add **commas** where they are needed.

We tiptoed nervously into the dark dank room. Arjun who was carrying the torch went ahead. As he swung the beam around we could see piles of books broken furniture paintings tilted at drunken angles and what looked like a heap of rusting machine parts in the corner.

Although it was obvious that Mr Pankhurst hadn't been in the room for years I somehow felt his presence still. In my head I could hear his voice puzzled yet stern asking us what we thought we were doing.

'I don't like this Arjun,' I whispered. 'It's creepy isn't it?'

BRACKETS AND DASHES

Brackets and **dashes** are often used to add extra information to sentences. **Hyphens** are used to join some compound words and to indicate words that are split between two lines on a page.

1 Add **round brackets** to part of each sentence. Add any other **punctuation** that is needed. The first one has been done for you.

a) The characters except for Rob are all in their thirties.

The characters (except for Rob) are all in their thirties.

b) You will be working with both Xena have you met her and Finn.

c) Have you seen Clara's house the one in Manchester

d) Lars has lost so much weight over three stone just by cutting out sugar.

e) She is a well known singer in Egypt.

2 Write ✓ or ✗ in the boxes to indicate if the **dashes** in these sentences are correct:

a) Our bodies function best from 35.5°–37.5°.   ☐

b) The colour of the water – a muddy green – was not attractive.   ☐

c) Travellers in the 75 – 85 age range require extra insurance.   ☐

d) Birgit was disappointed – that their old house was no longer there.   ☐

3 Are the **hyphens** in these words in an appropriate place if the word was split between two lines? Tick those that are. If they are not, write the word with the hyphen in a better place. There may be more than one possibility.

a) info-rmation   ☐   ....

b) narra-tive   ☐   ....

c) assonan-ce   ☐   ....

d) oxy-moron   ☐   ....

e) bea-utiful   ☐   ....

4 Add **hyphens** to these sentences if they are needed:

a) I use a news app in order to get up to date information.

b) The coffee machine was out of order.

c) The children were very badly behaved.

d) We were unable to make any long term plans.

APOSTROPHES

Apostrophes are used for two main reasons: to show possession in phrases ('Orwell's novel') and to represent missing letters in contracted words ('don't', 'I've').

1 Add **apostrophes** to these sentences where they are needed:

    a) The childrens diet consisted mainly of potatoes.

    b) Rays car was parked at the top of the hill, next to Glorias.

    c) Have you seen all the photos on Hamzas Facebook page?

    d) Marco is playing drums in Laura and Kits band now.

    e) Mrs Joness dog attacked Rogers cat.

2 Change the underlined part of the sentence to a form with an **apostrophe** unless it sounds unnatural to do so. The first one has been done for you.

    a) Has anyone seen <u>the laptop that belongs to Julio</u>?   _Julio's laptop_

    b) There was chaos when <u>the website of the company</u> crashed.

    c) I borrowed <u>the coat that James owns.</u>

    d) <u>The front door of their house</u> was painted bright yellow.

    e) Is this <u>the cat of Ellie and Brandon?</u>

3 Underline any words in this excerpt that could be written in a **contracted form**. Write the corrected paragraphs in the space provided.

> Farah was nervous. She had never given a speech in public before and she did not know whether she would be able to keep her voice steady.
>
> 'Do not worry,' her friend Robyn reassured her. 'It will be fine. Remember, you are the expert in this subject. You have done so much research for this talk. It is bound to be interesting.'

4 Complete the words in these sentences with a **contraction**. The first one has been done for you.

    a) I was surprised to see Ben there – I thought he'd left the previous day.

    b) I'm sorry, but you can take photographs in here.

    c) Karl and Leanne will call in if they got time.

    d) If you don't work a bit harder, you fail your exams.

    e) We can go swimming if it sunny tomorrow.

    f) I think it be easier to get to school when you have a bike.

5 Add any missing **apostrophes** to these sentences and cross out any that should not be there:

    a) Im not sure who'se shoes these are, but they may be Pauls.

    b) The elephant's owner's wash him every day.

    c) Davids not allowed to go in his parent's room.

    d) You can have some of Saras biscuit's if you're hungry.

    e) They've already met each others' families'.

    f) That bag is Elenas, not your's.

6 Rewrite these sentences using **contracted forms** wherever possible.
Add **apostrophes** where they are needed. The first one has been done for you.

    a) We have bought bunk beds for the twins room.

       We've bought bunk beds for the twins' room.

    b) We could go to Michels house if you would like to.

    c) Both of Dawn and Joes children were born in the 90s.

    d) Lets watch the womens football on TV tomorrow.

    e) You had better give Craigs book back now.

    f) We will see them later – they will be at the party.

COLONS AND SEMICOLONS

Colons and **semicolons** are used to separate parts of sentences. They indicate a slightly more definite break than a comma, but a slightly less definite one than a full stop.

1 Put a tick (✓) or cross (✗) in each box to indicate whether the **colon** is used correctly in these sentences:

a) The poem uses imagery from nature such as: budding flowers to symbolise new love. ☐

b) There was only one thing on Igor's mind: he wanted revenge. ☐

c) The following meal options are available: chicken curry, vegetarian lasagne, fish pie. ☐

d) If there is a medical emergency: call this number immediately. ☐

e) We must not forget the historical context of this novel: the war had only just ended. ☐

f) The trees are described as 'budding': however, the poem is set in winter. ☐

2 Add a **colon** or a **semicolon** to these sentences where appropriate. Sometimes both might be appropriate.

a) Mr Harris was only interested in one thing cricket.

b) My mother loved the idea of living in the countryside my father disagreed.

c) The scenery was spectacular snow-capped mountains towered above us.

d) Welcome drinks 7.30 p.m.

e) Macbeth is drawn to further evil after murdering Duncan he kills his guards.

f) Train times are as follows 10.30 for Exeter and 11.25 for Leeds.

3 Rewrite these sentences, adding **colons** and **semicolons** to make them clear:

a) Make sure you have the following items a waterproof coat thick socks and gloves a torch.

....

....

....

b) Activities included in the price are arts and crafts paintballing abseiling swimming.

....

....

....

c) The following foods are available from the campsite shop fruit and veg fresh and frozen meat or fish crisps and confectionery.

....

....

....

EFFECTIVE SPEECH PUNCTUATION

When writing speech, you should use **inverted commas** (' '). It is important to make sure that other punctuation marks, such as commas and full stops, are in the right places in written speech.

Remember:

● Only use speech marks or inverted commas for the actual words spoken.
● The first word spoken by a new speaker should have a capital letter.
● Punctuation before the word 'said' comes inside the speech marks.
● Start a new line (and indent it) whenever the speaker in a conversation changes.

1 Decide which of these sentences need **inverted commas**. Write ✓ if they do and ✗ if they do not.

a) Kiko asked me to go with her.   ☐

b) My teacher said that I needed to buy a revision guide.   ☐

c) Immie suddenly screamed, I need help!   ☐

d) It's raining outside, said Priya glumly.   ☐

2 Rewrite these sentences using correct **speech punctuation**:

a) 'Hi, Larry'! shouted Hal. 'how are you?'

....

b) 'I've never been to Africa' Shania said 'I'd love to go there.'

....

c) 'You must not leave the room', the examiner instructed. 'Unless there is an emergency'

....

d) Iman whispered 'I've got a secret to tell you'.

....

3 Rewrite these sentences using **direct speech**. The first one has been done for you.

a) She asked if I was hungry.

'Are you hungry?' she asked.

b) He said he was a teacher.

....

c) He asked if he could come in.

....

d) She exclaimed that she was absolutely freezing.

....

e) He said he'd like a sandwich.

....

4 Rewrite these sentences, adding **speech punctuation**:

a) Do you have a coat Rowena asked it's cold outside.

....

b) He won twenty thousand pounds Grace shrieked that's more than I earn in a year.

....

c) Baz said I don't like jazz much, do you?

....

d) The bus is waiting said our guide we are leaving in five minutes.

....

e) My boss David said is not going to like this!

....

5 Read the following paragraph and then:

- Mark any points where you think speech marks or other punctuation should go
- Rewrite the paragraph in the space provided, adding speech punctuation

The woman in red robes took us to the castle gate. Be careful she said the forest is a dangerous place. Are there bears asked Ryan in a small voice. There aren't any bears she said but there are snakes. They don't often bite people, but when they do, few survive. I put an arm around Ryan's shoulder. He looked deathly pale. Don't worry I said we're going to be fine, I know we are. The woman shrugged. Let's hope so she said doubtfully.

....

....

....

....

....

....

....

....

....

....

TEST YOUR UNDERSTANDING

Rewrite this extract from a student's piece of creative writing, correcting any **punctuation** errors. (There are no spelling or grammar errors.)

Ask yourself these questions:

● Are the punctuation marks appropriate for the function the writer intends?
● Are they all in the correct position?
● Are there any punctuation marks missing?
● Does the text start a new line when it needs to?

It was the end of another long boring day, Tara and her brother Josh had been sitting at the window for hours, waiting for the sound of their parents car coming up the long drive. Although they were only eight and six the children were used to being left alone. After all, what other choice was there.

If their parents did'nt go to the factory every day there wouldn't be any money to buy food. The Grand Master who controlled all their lives saw to that. The children didn't like it but they were used to it. They weren't usually scared to be left alone. However today was different. Today they were definitely scared. 'They should be home by now' said Josh in a quavery voice, 'I don't like it'! 'I'm sure they won't be long?' Tara reassured him, but in reality she was far from certain.

They had never been this late before, in her heart, she knew that something was wrong. Everything had been strange that morning. Even the bird's who usually sang to greet the day had been silent in the eerie, grey dawn.

....

....

....

....

....

....

....

....

....

....

....

USING PARAGRAPHS EFFECTIVELY

A **paragraph** is a section of text that starts on a new line, a little indented from the edge, which contains at least one sentence. It usually deals with a single theme or idea.

USING PARAGRAPHS IN CREATIVE WRITING

In stories, writers use new paragraphs in several ways – for example, to introduce a new character to the story.

1 The underlined words in these sentences represent the start of paragraphs in different stories. Match each one with a reason for the new paragraph listed in the box below. The first one has been done for you.

a) Grateful to see a familiar face at the gathering, Laura approached her neighbour and complimented her on her dress.

  <u>Standing in the opposite corner of the room was a slight young man</u> dressed in black.

  Reason: A new character is introduced to the story.

b) Paolo said goodbye to his mother and promised to call her the next week. He could never quite shake the feeling of guilt after their phone conversations.

  <u>Patting his back pocket</u> to check his wallet was there, he left the house.

  Reason: ....

c) The conversation with Luca hadn't gone well. After five long minutes, Sara had wound it up. She went to her bed, discouraged.

  <u>The next morning</u> she woke with a nagging sense of unfinished business.

  Reason: ....

d) Reason: 'Anyway, I thought we could catch a film later, if you fancied it?'

  <u>'Oh sure, yeah I'm up for that.'</u>

  Reason: ....

e) Spying her friend in the café, Aisha immediately abandoned her plans to head to the library and pushed open the door.

  <u>At home, Ethan stretched out on the sofa,</u> a paper in his hand. The whole house seemed to breathe a sigh of relief when Aisha left.

  Reason: ....

> *A different idea, topic or event is being described.*
> *A different character's thoughts or actions are being described.*
> ~~*A new character is introduced to the story.*~~
> *There is a time shift in the action being described.*
> *The speaker in a dialogue has changed.*

2 Read the text and decide where **paragraphs** should go. Then:

- Insert two slanted lines (//) to show the place you think they need adding
- Rewrite the text, with the paragraphs clearly shown, in the space below

She noticed that he was looking tired and somewhat dishevelled, his hair lank and unwashed and his skin faintly pallid. Without warning, he crouched down to retrieve something from the canvas bag that lay at his feet and then stood up, with an air of triumph. 'This is for you, Naomi!' he announced, brandishing a crumpled letter. 'For me? What?' she replied, seemingly baffled at this development. 'Yes, you'll understand once you've read it. It'll all make sense – trust me.' He turned on his heel and walked away. 'Antonio, wait! I need to speak to you. Don't go!' 'Sorry, I'm due somewhere else now. You'll be fine – you'll see,' he replied, walking backwards to face her as he said it. Later that afternoon, in the privacy of her bedroom and with trembling hands, Naomi ripped open the envelope.

USING PARAGRAPHS IN PERSUASIVE WRITING

In the 'main body' of a persuasive essay (i.e. the middle part), writers usually use **paragraphs** to make different points. Each paragraph conveys a new point or focus.

3 Create three **paragraphs** in the following extract by indicating with two lines (//) where you would start new paragraphs.

There is a great deal of concern over the amount of time that young people are spending on their screens, be it mobile phones, tablets or laptops. Admittedly, a cursory glance around a café or other public place will reveal a significant proportion of people under twenty-five consulting a screen. Similarly, most parents nowadays will testify that it is sometimes a battle to persuade their offspring to put down their mobile phone during mealtimes. However, this is certainly not the whole story. Let us consider for a moment, what those young people are doing with their screens. Some of them will be 'chatting' with friends. It may not be 'face time' conversation, but it is conversation nonetheless, with all the pleasures and benefits that that brings. After all, anything that mitigates the loneliness of twenty-first century existence has some merit. Others, meanwhile, will be consuming social media which, contrary to its popular image, is not dominated solely by pictures of kittens and puppies. Indeed social media is the medium through which many young people learn about current affairs, and there is more and more evidence to suggest that they are learning a considerable amount. Certainly if public marches are a barometer of youthful political engagement, this would seem to be the case.

TOPIC SENTENCES

A **topic sentence** gives the reader the main idea of a paragraph. It usually (but not always) comes at the start of the paragraph.

4 Underline three **topic sentences** in the following extract and indicate with two lines where you would start new **paragraphs:**

All school-leavers should take a gap year

Travel broadens the mind, it is said. A cliché this may be but, like all clichés, there is an element of truth to it. Many teenagers entering adulthood will only have lived in one country, or even one area of a country. Accordingly, however positive their experience of life, it will inevitably be limited. Overseas travel introduces young people to other languages, cultures and ways of life. This has the effect of opening up the mind to other ways of being in a way that is stimulating and enriching. It benefits young people to be challenged. Very often, young people have lived sheltered lives in families where parents have made their arrangements and dealt with their problems. Though perfectly natural, this parent-child dynamic does not always equip young adults to deal with the rigours of modern life. Travel pulls young people out of their comfort zone and forces them to develop basic life skills. Airports and railways stations must be negotiated, strangers approached for information, food purchased, and very often, all in a different language. This is hugely character-building. We learn to appreciate our homes. Most of us have grown up in centrally heated houses, with an array of electrical appliances at our disposal. Overseas travel on a budget is not always comfortable. Indeed, it can be quite gruelling. Consequently, we often return with a heightened appreciation of our homes and neighbourhoods.

HOW TO USE CONNECTIVES

Connectives are words and phrases that link or show contrast between ideas within a piece of writing.

1 Draw lines to match the common **connectives** in each group with their function in a sentence or paragraph:

a) likewise, equally, in the same way

b) overall, on the whole

c) for this reason, with this in mind

d) in contrast, conversely, however

e) for instance, namely, notably

f) in addition, also, furthermore

giving a specific example

linking a similar idea

adding to an idea

presenting a different idea

showing something's purpose

generalising

2 Circle the **connective** that works best in each of these sentences:

a) Miriam was tall, dark and willowy. [Similarly / By way of contrast], her sister was short and heavily built, with fair hair.

b) The past decade has seen a marked increase in the number of diet-related illnesses, [most notably / as a result] obesity and type 2 diabetes.

c) Burcu found the monotonous landscape and the grey skies depressing. [Moreover / Accordingly], she missed her family and friends and was desperate to see them again.

d) The fact remains that the Internet is an extraordinary source of information. [For this reason / On the other hand], we should value it.

e) The problem, if anything, is worsening. The government's strategy to fix it is [evidently / consequently] not working.

f) We shouldn't lose hope: [on the whole / equally] the situation looks positive.

3 Draw lines to match the two halves of these sentences:

a) As a leader, she is courageous, calm and analytical. Furthermore,

b) Some regard her as too tolerant and caring while conversely,

c) Her critics say that she has failed in some key areas, specifically

d) She is good at dealing with conflict and is therefore

e) She is very logical, but equally

f) Her serious nature can be a disadvantage – for example,

some see her as not compassionate enough.

she is able to inspire confidence.

some have criticised her humourless speeches.

particularly able to lead in these troubled times.

energy and the environment.

she often comes up with creative solutions.

4 Complete these sentences using the most suitable **connective** from the box below:

a) The theatre is a very splendid building and evidently recently restored.

...., the apartments next to it are shabby and down-at-heel.

b) Of course, we must take into account the views of older people but

...., we must listen to what young people have to say.

c) Unlike his sister, Raj wasn't sociable and outgoing. ...., he could be shy and tended to prefer his own company to that of others.

d) She was struck by the rugged beauty of the landscape, ... the mountains in the west.

e) He was in hospital for much of his childhood and ...., missed out on a great deal of schooling.

equally	in particular	as a result
indeed	in stark contrast	

5 In each pair of sentences, tick (✓) the one that shows the correct underlined **connective**:

a) A punitive tax could be put in place to penalise this harmful practice. <u>Alternatively,</u> we could provide tax incentives to businesses who do not pollute in this way. ☐

A punitive tax could be put in place to penalise this harmful practice. <u>Consequently,</u> we could provide tax incentives to businesses who do not pollute in this way. ☐

b) Her background was very privileged, <u>whereas</u> his had been poor. ☐

Her background was very privileged, <u>nevertheless</u> his had been poor. ☐

c) She found the task difficult and at times thankless. <u>Moreover,</u> she persevered and, in the end, succeeded. ☐

She found the task difficult and at times thankless. <u>Nevertheless,</u> she persevered and, in the end, succeeded. ☐

d) The scheme was pointless. It was unlikely that it would succeed. <u>Besides,</u> it was too expensive. ☐

The scheme was pointless. It was unlikely that it would succeed. <u>Hence,</u> it was too expensive. ☐

e) The global population is increasing; <u>conversely,</u> the need for greater food supplies. ☐

The global population is increasing; <u>hence</u> the need for greater food supplies. ☐

TEST YOUR UNDERSTANDING

Read this letter of complaint to a local newspaper. Rewrite the letter in the space on page 47. Divide the text into four paragraphs and add the connectives in the box below to make the text flow. (Use each connective once.)

Dear Sir/Madam,

I was disappointed to read a review of city-centre cafés in your newspaper (11th March), which failed to feature a single vegetarian or vegan café .... the existence of several in the city centre. As a long-time vegetarian who has recently turned vegan, I am saddened by this omission and would like to share my thoughts with you. .... I would like to point out the sheer number of non meat-eaters in the city. Whether for ethical, environmental or health reasons, over five per cent of the population of this country now chooses not to eat meat. This represents a considerable number of people. ...., the figure is set to increase dramatically with the vegan movement now going mainstream. ...., would it not make sense to include establishments that cater for this large group of people in your round-up of the city's cafés? Ironically, your café round-up was featured on the same page as an article encouraging us all to practise 'green, urban living', quite rightly extolling the virtues of practices .... cycling, recycling, etc. As a newspaper, you are .... very much in favour of environmental initiatives. Indeed, this is partly why I read your paper. ...., in the same spread, you miss the opportunity to tell people about the cafés in the city where they can eat sustainably. (For anyone who is interested, Café Rainbow on Hill Street is one such establishment, The Pod (Lawrence Street) and Friends' Café (Montreal Road) are two others.)

............................, I would like to draw to your attention the upcoming Vegan Fair at the City Community College, 5th May. I look forward to seeing coverage of this exciting event in your newspaper.

Yours faithfully,
Jo Lynch

despite	however	such as	firstly
moreover	finally	evidently	with this in mind

TASK

Introduction

In this section you will have the chance to complete a GCSE-style writing task, similar to ones you might face in the exam.

- Use the write-in space to start the task.
- Then check each of the three sample responses at different levels to assess your progress.

Your task

> **Write the opening part of a story in which someone goes on an exciting journey.**

Write as much as you can in the space provided and continue on separate sheets if necessary.

As you write, ask yourself the following questions:

- Have I used a wide and interesting range of vocabulary?
- Is my spelling accurate?
- Have I used a range of sentence types to ensure a good style?
- Is my grammar accurate? Do all the verbs agree with their subjects?
- Have I used direct speech to develop the story? Is it punctuated accurately?
- Have I used paragraphs effectively?

When you have finished writing, check your work and make any corrections that are needed.

SAMPLE ANSWERS

Look at each of the following sample responses at different levels, then read the commentaries that follow them. Make your own judgement as to how close you are to each one in terms of their use of spelling, punctuation and grammar. Note that the numbers shown in each commentary are examples. They are not a complete list of all the features in the text.

Student A

The airoplane [1] was above the clouds. Jenny couldn't relax. She was scared of flying. The captain had just put on the fasten seatbelts sign and that made her even more nervouser. [2] [6] Sure enough, they were soon being tossed around. Even the flight attendents [1] couldn't stand up. They had to sit down to [1]. Ahmer who was sitting next to her didn't seem bothered. [10] He was playing a video game on his laptop. Suddenly something happened that were even more scary than the storm outside. [5] A young woman in a red jumper stood up and took a gun out of her handbag!!!! [8]

'Ahmer look!' Jenny cried. She grabbed Ahmers arm. [11] 'Get off me,' Ahmer said angryly [1]. Jenny grabbed his arm even tighter. He looked at her face. When he saw her face he realised that something really was wrong. [3] Now Jenny could see that Ahmer was as scared as she was. She looked around the plane. Not everyone had noticed the woman yet. But the ones who had were silent, they didn't know what to do. [9]

Everyone was waiting for the woman to say something or to do something. Jenny felt like her hart [1] would burst. It was beating so hard. Eventually the woman spoke. 'You! she commanded pointing at an old man. [15] 'Take this box around the cabin. Everyone must throw there [1] phones in it. If I find anyone with a phone they will be shot.' By now some people was begining [1] to cry. [5] Including Ahmer. [4] Jenny had never seen him cry before. 'Don't cry Ahmer,' she said 'its [12] going to be OK.' The poor man with the box was having a lot of dificulty [1] getting round the plane because the storm was still continuing and the floor was tipping from side to side. [3] Jenny realised she has forgotten to be scared of the storm! [7] Then the woman with the gun spoke to one of the attendents. [1] 'Tell the captain to change our coarse [1] to Chicago.' 'We don't have enough fuel.' said the attendant. 'I don't beleive you' [1] said the woman. [14] Jenny thought they were going to end up crashing in the sea. She thought about her parent's [13] and about her little dog Jack waiting for her at home. [2] She didn't cry like Ahmer though. In fact she felt quite calm in a wierd [1] way. But then the woman with the gun walked over and pointed it at her. [16]

LOWER LEVEL

COMMENTARY

- **Overview:** The text can be followed but the errors create some misunderstandings and the text is not as fluent as it might be.
- Vocabulary is appropriate but the range is very limited.
- There is some accurate spelling, but there are also several errors [1].
- There are some compound [2] and complex [3] sentences, but there are too many simple sentences, so the narrative does not flow smoothly. More ambitious sentence types, such as minor sentences or rhetorical questions, are not used. A sentence fragment is used inappropriately [4].
- Grammar is mostly accurate but there are some errors, for example with subject and verb agreement [5], forming a comparative [6] and choosing the correct tense [7].
- Basic punctuation is mainly correct. There is inappropriate use of multiple exclamation marks [8]. There are several higher-level punctuation errors, such as the comma splice [9], lack of commas for a relative clause [10] and lack of apostrophes for possession [11] and contractions [12]. There is a plural that wrongly includes an apostrophe. [13]
- Speech punctuation is not always accurate [14] and speech does not always start a new line where needed. [15]
- Paragraphs are mostly used effectively, but there is one paragraph that should be divided, both for speech and because the scene changes. [16]

Student B

I sat down on one of the seats in our compartment. **[3]** Outside, there was total cahos **[2]** on the station platform as hundreds of people swarmed **[1]** onto the train, dragging huge suitcases and screaming children. **[5]** Beside me, the woman who had come to my apartment that morning opened a newspaper and started to read.

I was puzzled. **[3]** I could see people pushing their way down the corridor and argueing **[2]** over seats in loud voices. **[4]** However, nobody tried to come into our compartment, it seemed as if they knew there was something strange about us. **[9]**

I looked again at the woman next to me. She had thin chekes **[2]** and pale skin. Her hair was mostly covered with a green hat, but a few black hairs came down over her face. **[4]** Suddenly she looked up from her newspaper. Her eyes, which seemed to be looking right into my brain, was an icy grey. **[6] [7]** 'If anyone comes in, let me do the talking' she said in an unfriendly voice. **[11]**

'Where are we going?' I asked 'what's happening? Who are you?' **[10]**

The woman sniffed. 'If you want to stay safe, your **[2]** going to have to learn not to ask so many questions,' she hissed. **[1]** 'Just sit there and be quiet. You'll find out where we're going when we get there.' Eventually the train started to move. I could hear voices from the crowded compartments around us, but we were still alone. The train moved slowly through the outskirts of the city. I looked up at the huge, ugly apartment blocks. **[8]** Sometimes I could see people standing on their balconys **[2]** and I wanted to be up there with them not on this train heading for a place I didn't know with this strange and scary woman. After a while we left the city behind and got faster as we went through the countryside. Fields with cows and horses, farmers on their tractors and little cottages with gardens full of flowers flew past our windows. They all looked so normal but inside the compartment nothing was normal at all. 'At least tell me your name,' I said to the woman. 'You can call me Lena,' she said. **[12]**

I was beginning to feel hungry, but I hadn't brought any food with me, just my passport and a few clothes, as Lena had told me to. I couldn't imagine where she was taking me, but I knew that it wouldn't be anywhere I wanted to go.

MID LEVEL

COMMENTARY

- **Overview:** The text is mostly clear but a few issues with layout and small spelling errors interrupt the flow in places.
- Vocabulary is appropriate and there are instances of vocabulary used for impact **[1]**, but overall the vocabulary range is rather limited.
- Spelling is mostly accurate, with a few errors **[2]**.
- A good range of basic sentence types has been used, including simple **[3]**, compound **[4]** and complex sentences **[5]**. More ambitious sentence types such as minor sentences or rhetorical questions are not used.
- Grammar is mostly accurate. There is one instance where the verb does not agree with the subject **[6]**.

- Punctuation is mostly accurate and includes some high-level uses such as commas for a relative clause **[7]** and between adjectives **[8]**. There are some errors, including a comma splice **[9]** and several errors in speech punctuation **[10]**.
- Speech does not always start a new line where needed. **[11]**
- Paragraphs are mostly used effectively, but there is one paragraph that should be divided, both for speech and because the scene changes. **[12]**

Student C

It seemed like a good idea at the time **[2]**.

'Let's climb Ben Nevis!' Reece cried. 'It's the highest mountain in the UK. It'd be so cool!'

'But that's in Scotland.'

Reece gave me one of his special looks. One of those looks that combined amusement and contempt. **[5]**

'Yes,' he said slowly, as if speaking to a rather dim child. 'I know it's in Scotland.'

'But we live in London.'

'I know where we live, Kendra!'

'So how are we going to get to Scotland?'

Reece had a plan. Of course he did! Reece was one of those people who always had plans. His head was constantly full of them, jiggling and jostling around **[1]**. No wonder his teachers complained that he never concentrated in class. But me? I was the quiet, practical one. I was the one that worried about what other people would think, the one that craved security, the one – as Reece would say – that created problems out of nothing. **[7]**

So how come I agreed to this crazy plan? **[6]** Maybe it was because the summer holidays stretched ahead in a long, hot line of boredom. Mum and Dad were both up to their eyes in work as usual, so there was no chance of a family holiday. **[3]** Maybe it was simply the idea of getting out of the dull grime of the city and into the fresh countryside. Maybe it was because Mum and Dad said we'd never make it.

Whatever the reason, on the first weekend of the school holidays, I found myself in my room, a huge pile of stuff on my bed, puzzling over how to fit even half of it into my bike panniers. Yes, we were going by bike – all the way to Scotland! Never mind that the furthest I'd ever ridden was to my friend Maddie's house three miles away.

We set off in the rain, which was not a very auspicious start. **[1]** I couldn't believe how heavy my bike felt, all loaded up like that. Despite his skinny frame, Reece seemed to have no trouble powering ahead of me. **[4]**

It seemed to me that the city would never end. On and on we went, through streets that all looked the same – the same shops, the same people, mechanically going about their business, the same vans delivering goods, the same litter on the pavements. I began to think we must be going round and round in circles.

The muscles in my thighs were burning and my saddle was so uncomfortable, I had to keep standing up to pedal. Eventually Reece pulled over by a bench.

'How far have we come?' I panted. 'Are we nearly out of London yet?'

Reece glanced at his satnav and laughed. 'Well done Kendra – this is the furthest you've ever cycled!'

A warm glow of pride spread through my body, but before I'd had time to congratulate myself, he spoiled it all.

'Yes, you've done a massive four miles! Only another forty till we get to the youth hostel.'

HIGHER LEVEL

COMMENTARY

- **Overview**: The text is very clearly laid out and fluently written, supporting the ideas and communicating them in an interesting way.
- A good range of ambitious and appropriate vocabulary has been used **[1]**.
- Spelling is accurate.
- A range of sentence types has been used, including simple **[2]**, compound **[3]** and complex sentences **[4]**, sentence fragments have been used for effect **[5]** and rhetorical questions included **[6]**.
- Grammar is accurate and verbs agree with their subject.
- Punctuation is accurate and includes some ambitious uses, such as dashes **[7]**.
- Speech is punctuated accurately and starts a new line where needed.
- Paragraphs are used effectively to indicate a change of time, focus, etc.

PART ONE: HOW GOOD IS YOUR SPAG?

SPAG CHECK (page 6)

1. a) apparent
   b) privilege
   c) persistent
   d) definitely
   e) weird
   f) admittedly
   g) awful
   h) parallel
   i) heroes

2. a) verb
   b) noun
   c) pronoun
   d) adjective
   e) adverb
   f) preposition
   g) conjunction
   h) determiner

3. a) A
   b) C
   c) C
   d) P
   e) A
   f) P
   g) C

4. a) ✗ broken
   b) ✗ shown
   c) ✗ drawn
   d) ✗ beaten
   e) ✓
   f) ✗ shaken
   g) ✗ drunk
   h) ✗ begun

5. a) Even though she has plenty of money, she still complains.
   b) My sister, who never takes any exercise, still managed to run faster than me!
   c) She handed him a small, black box.
   d) Could you come here, Otis?
   e) Similarly, temperatures may vary quite considerably.
   f) You've been to Mexico, haven't you?
   g) Madrid, which is the capital of Spain, is in the middle of the country.
   h) It's hot in here, isn't it?

6. a) ✗ its
   b) ✗ women's
   c) ✗ children's
   d) ✓
   e) ✗ tomatoes
   f) ✓
   g) ✗ yours
   h) ✓

TEST YOUR UNDERSTANDING (page 8)

As he steps out on to the street, he feels a heat that is more intense <u>than</u> [1] anything he can remember. He has never been <u>hotter</u> [2]. <u>It is</u> [3] oppressive and unrelenting, and all but takes his breath away. He makes his way, slowly, to the market square. The square is seething with people, eager to catch a glimpse of the dancers. Intrigued, he joins them, weaving his way in. As if from nowhere, a blizzard of crimson petals and torn fragments of paper suddenly <u>descends</u> [4], turning the air momentarily <u>pink. It</u> [5] comes slowly to rest on the heads and shoulders of the eager onlookers. A young girl next to him, her eyes round with wonder, <u>disappears</u> [6] into the crowd as if sucked in by an irresistible force. Somewhere beyond the wall of bodies, someone beats out a <u>rhythm</u> [7] on the drums, sending a ripple of excitement through the crowd. He strains every nerve to see <u>past</u> [8] the wall of people in front of him, but to no avail. There are just <u>too</u> [9] many bodies. He gives in to the will of the crowd and lets himself be buffeted one way and then another. He looks up. Above him, the sky is a watercolour painting of <u>pink, red and orange</u> [10].

[1] The word that the student intended here is 'than' not 'then'. For comparisons, 'than' is the correct word.

[2] The student should have written 'hotter' (without 'more'). Adjectives such as 'hot', which have one syllable, usually form their comparatives by adding '-er'.

[3] The student should have written 'It is' or used the contracted form 'It's'. Instead, they have mistakenly used the possessive determiner 'its' (used correctly in sentences such as 'The river had burst its banks').

[4] An 's' is missing here. The word is spelt 'descends'.

[5] A new sentence is needed here. The student has mistakenly run two sentences together, making a mistake known as a 'comma splice'.

[6] 'Disappear' is spelt with one 's' and two 'p's.

[7] 'Rhythm' contains the silent letter 'h'.

[8] The word required here is 'past', not 'passed' (which is the past tense of the verb 'pass'). To convey the sense of 'beyond a certain point in time or place', we need the word 'past'.

[9] The adverb 'too' is needed here, meaning 'excessively'. The student has confused this word with the common preposition 'to'.

[10] A comma is needed here between the words 'pink' and 'red'. Commas are used to separate items in a list of three or more people or things. Generally, in a list like this, a comma is not needed before 'and'.

PART TWO: SPELLINGS FOR SUCCESS

COMMON SPELLING ERRORS (page 9)

1. a) station<u>a</u>ry
   b) appar<u>e</u>nt
   c) accept<u>a</u>ble
   d) privi<u>le</u>ge
   e) separ<u>a</u>te
   f) defin<u>ite</u>ly

2 a) necessary
b) dessert
c) address
d) dilemma
e) Admittedly
f) successful

3 a) familiar
b) persistent
c) relevant
d) accommodation / because
e) parallels / analogous
f) embarrassed

4 a) argument
b) gauge
c) completely
d) liaison
e) accidentally
f) noticeable

5 a) ✗ cemetery
b) ✓
c) ✗ colleagues
d) ✗ definitely
e) ✗ publicly

6 a) occasion
b) independent
c) appearance
d) bizarre
e) curiosity
f) conscious

SPELLING STRATEGIES (page 11)

1 a) <u>we</u>ird
b) hier<u>ar</u>chy
c) bus<u>ine</u>ss
d) indepen<u>dent</u>
e) env<u>iron</u>ment
f) fri<u>en</u>ds

2 a) unfortun<u>ate</u>ly
b) know<u>ledge</u>
c) ten<u>den</u>cy
d) <u>fur</u>ther
e) accept<u>able</u>

3 a) calendar
b) mystery
c) category
d) reference
e) controversy

USEFUL WORDS FOR ENGLISH (page 12)

1 a) character
b) rhythm
c) syllable
d) euphemism
e) parallel
f) nonetheless

2 a) rep<u>eti</u>tion
b) den<u>oue</u>ment
c) onomatop<u>oe</u>ic
d) omni<u>scie</u>nt
e) contemp<u>orary</u>
f) prot<u>ago</u>nist

3 a) opposed
b) believe
c) maintain
d) Admittedly
e) undoubtedly

LETTER ORDER, SILENT LETTERS AND PLURALS (page 13)

1 a) ach<u>ie</u>ved
b) rec<u>ei</u>ved
c) for<u>ei</u>gn
d) glac<u>ie</u>rs
e) f<u>ei</u>gned
f) s<u>ei</u>zed

2 a) <u>k</u>nowledge
b) w<u>h</u>ispered
c) rus<u>t</u>led
d) reigned
e) <u>k</u>nocked
f) campai<u>g</u>ned

3 a) ✗ bombed
b) ✗ rhyme
c) ✓
d) ✗ fastened

4 a) dresses
b) heroes
c) halves
d) beliefs
e) criteria
f) series
g) quizzes
h) echoes

5 a) tomatoes
b) countries
c) roofs
d) knives
e) discos
f) deer
g) runners-up
h) volcanoes

6 a) leaves
b) flies
c) branches
d) lives

COMMONLY CONFUSED WORDS (page 15)

1
a) affect
b) except
c) bear
d) brake
e) lose
f) illusion
g) breathe

2
a) break
b) bare
c) loose
d) past
e) than
f) complimented
g) dessert

3
a) ✗ too
b) ✗ passed
c) ✗ than
d) ✓
e) ✗ break
f) ✓
g) ✗ have

PREFIXES AND SUFFIXES (page 16)

1
a) un- = opposite to
b) mis- = wrongly or badly
c) re- = again
d) pre- = before
e) dis- = not
f) over- = too much

2
a) dissimilar
b) boredom
c) awful
d) misshapen
e) stopping
f) becoming
g) ugliness

3
a) <u>mis</u>spelt
b) gap<u>ing</u>
c) <u>dis</u>satisfied
d) chat<u>ted</u>
e) cop<u>ing</u>
f) <u>un</u>fair
g) grate<u>ful</u>

4
a) reproachful
b) hoping
c) attentiveness
d) patted

TEST YOUR UNDERSTANDING (page17)

Sylvie sidled <u>past</u> a cluster of people and made for the exit. No one was looking. She <u>fastened</u> her coat and slipped out of the church through <u>its</u> hefty wooden door. Checking first that it was deserted, she headed to the churchyard. The snow and old <u>leaves </u>had been brushed from the paving stones and what now remained underfoot was a slick of ice that made walking almost impossible. She made her way gingerly, steadying herself against the wall of the church with one <u>bare</u> hand till her fingers were <u>numb</u> with cold. The ancient yew tree that crouched over the gravestones was laden with snow. Its <u>branches</u> hung low with the sheer <u>weight</u> of frozen water. Suddenly smitten by the snow's eerie beauty in the dim light, Sylvie stopped to gaze around her. Yesterday's weather <u>forecast</u> had promised overnight snow and when she woke this morning, her whole room was suffused by a pinkish light, Sylvie had not been <u>disappointed</u>.

PART THREE: GET YOUR GRAMMAR RIGHT!

VOCABULARY FOR IMPACT (page 18)

1
a) diminish, shrink, dwindle
b) clutch, grasp, cling
c) surplus, excess, superfluous
d) supple, lithe, nimble
e) swift, rapid, brisk
f) suitable, apt, fitting

2
a) squalid
b) vast
c) ludicrous
d) petrified
e) meticulous
f) devastated

3
a) elitist
b) fawn over
c) garish
d) mollycoddle
e) smarmy
f) laughable

WHAT ARE WORD CLASSES? (page 19)

1

Nouns	walk, contentment, pride, export
Pronouns	it, them, who, each
Verbs	walk, describe, export, portray
Prepositions	underneath, over, on, from
Adjectives	ridiculous, fast, serious
Adverbs	quietly, hardly, fast, however
Conjunctions	and, but, or
Determiners	the, each, my

2 a) The play was first performed in the <u>soviet union</u> in 1946 and is one of <u>priestley's</u> best-known works.
   b) The actor <u>john gielgud</u> staged a version of *romeo and juliet* using <u>elizabethan</u> costumes.
   c) <u>Mr jones</u> is the original owner of <u>manor farm</u>, where *animal farm* is set.
   d) Papa is <u>daljit's</u> husband and he comes from <u>lahore</u> in what is now <u>pakistan</u>.

3 a) concrete, countable
   b) abstract, uncountable
   c) concrete, countable
   d) abstract, uncountable

4 a) you're
   b) I
   c) their, it's
   d) whose
   e) Your, its
   f) my
   g) They're

5 a) quickly
   b) easily
   c) reluctantly
   d) well
   e) politely
   f) doubtfully
   g) actively

6 a) politely
   b) doubtfully
   c) reluctant
   d) quickly
   e) well
   f) easily
   g) active

CLAUSES AND TYPES OF SENTENCES (page 21)

1 a) Our <u>teacher</u> <u>gave</u> us too much homework.
   b) The <u>car</u> <u>started</u> straight away.
   c) The <u>book</u> on the table <u>is</u> about African animals.
   d) Why don't <u>you</u> <u>give</u> the money to Jan?
   e) All of Maria's <u>children</u> <u>enjoy</u> playing tennis.

2 a) 2
   b) 3
   c) 1
   d) 1
   e) 2

3 a) M
   b) S
   c) M
   d) S
   e) M
   f) S

4 a) minor sentence
   b) compound sentence
   c) simple sentence
   d) complex sentence

5 a) 3, 4, 7
   b) 2, 6
   c) 5
   d) 1, 8

6 a) When Reeva saw the palace, she was amazed. (complex)
   b) Least said, soonest mended. (minor)
   c) Lukas gave Mira a beautiful glass vase for her birthday. (simple)
   d) Reading helps me relax, whereas yoga doesn't. (complex)

7 a) Although
   b) but
   c) When
   d) since
   e) unless
   f) if
   g) so

8 a) Meena's mother appears calm to the outside world although she sometimes has bad moods.
   b) Because she does not want to get into trouble, Meena tells lies.
   c) (Not possible)
   d) The animals cannot control the farm unless they get rid of the farmer.
   e) (Not possible)
   f) When the farmers launch an attack, Snowball orders the animals to retreat.

USING SENTENCES ACCURATELY (page 24)

1 (possible answers)
   a) The opening paragraph is extremely dramatic. It grabs the reader's interest.
   b) In this poem, the colour yellow is often associated with decay and red is associated with danger.
   c) ✓
   d) I was not able to join my friends at the cinema. I had too much work to do.
   e) ✓

2 a) so
   b) but
   c) because
   d) or

3 a) was
   b) is / was / has been
   c) has
   d) doesn't / does not / cannot
   e) has
   f) are

4 a) were
   b) want / wants
   c) emphasises
   d) is / are
   e) behave

5 a) was
   b) ✓
   c) are
   d) owes
   e) ✓
   f) ✓

TENSES AND MODAL VERBS (page 26)

1 a) had met
   b) is meeting
   c) met
   d) meets
   e) has met

2 a) forgot, forgotten
   b) built, built
   c) hid, hidden
   d) shrank, shrunk
   e) stole, stolen
   f) paid, paid
   g) thought, thought
   h) tore, torn

3 a) saw
   b) tries
   c) had escaped
   d) 'll/will come
   e) 've/have done

4 a) expressing certainty about the future
   b) expressing certainty about the past
   c) expressing ability
   d) expressing possibility
   e) expressing advice
   f) expressing an opinion

5 a) cannot
   b) could not
   c) must not
   d) shall not
   e) would not
   f) might not
   g) ought not to
   h) will not

6 a) wouldn't
   b) shouldn't / oughtn't to / mustn't
   c) mustn't
   d) mightn't
   e) won't
   f) oughtn't to / shouldn't
   g) couldn't

TEST YOUR UNDERSTANDING (page 28)

J. B. Priestley presents Sybil Birling as a very cold <u>*woman. This*</u> *[1] is because she thinks she is better than other people. She is outraged to be under suspicion, and particularly upset that the Inspector has interrupted* <u>*their*</u> *[2] party.*

In Act Two she tries to bully Sheila, telling her to go to bed. Then she <u>*starts*</u> *[3] to tell Inspector Goole off. She tells him that Mr Birling* <u>*was*</u> *[4] a mayor and a magistrate, saying, 'You know of course that my husband was Lord Mayor only two years ago' but [5] the Inspector takes no notice.*

Sybil Birling is a heartless person. She does not want to help the <u>*most poor/poorest*</u> *[6] people if she thinks they haven't earned [7] it. For example, she tells the Inspector they've been 'helping deserving cases'.* <u>*This*</u> *[8] means she* <u>*doesn't want*</u> *[9] to help people who, in her opinion, do not deserve it. In those days people had to rely* <u>*on*</u> *[10] charities because there* <u>*weren't*</u> *any [11] benefits from the government.*

[1] This is a run-on sentence so needs to be divided into two sentences as shown.

[2] The student misspelt the determiner 'their'.

[3] The tense suddenly changed – present tense should be maintained throughout, so this should be 'starts'.

[4] Subject and verb agreement error in the original – this should be 'was' not 'were'.

[5] Do not start sentences with 'and' or 'but' in formal writing. Use 'but' here as a conjunction to make a compound sentence.

[6] 'Most poorest' is incorrect. Ether 'more/most' or '-er', '-est' are needed to form comparatives and superlatives – not both.

[7] Incorrect past participle – 'earnt' should be 'earned'.

[8] This is a comma splice and needs either to be split into two sentences or joined with a conjunction.

[9] Error with the subject and verb agreement of the auxiliary verb.

[10] Wrong preposition used: 'on' is needed, not 'of'.

[11] Subject and verb agreement error.

PART FOUR: PUNCTUATION FOR ACCURACY AND EFFECT

FULL STOPS, QUESTION MARKS AND EXCLAMATION MARKS (page 29)

1 a) Karim won a million pounds in the lottery. What's he going to do with it?
   b) Emma wants to know if dinner's ready. Tell her it will be five minutes.
   c) What do you think of the painting? It's beautiful, isn't it?
   d) Would you ever go skydiving? Not in a million years!
   e) What did Sam say to you? He asked if I was going to the movie.
   f) Stay away from the edge of the cliff. Don't you know how dangerous it is?

2 a) His appointment with Dr. Millar was scheduled for 9 a.m. on Monday.
   b) Send it back to the firm you bought it from, i.e. Camburst Ltd. in Liverpool.
   c) Some of my favourite authors, e.g. A. A. Milne and C. S. Lewis, wrote for children.
   d) A lot of writers, artists etc. live in this street, and his home is No. 7.
   e) Prof. J. Cramer and Dr. V. González both work at the university.
   f) The Skills Corp. headquarters are located at 53 Acacia Ave., Newtown.

3 a) .
   b) .
   c) ?
   d) ?
   e) .
   f) ?

4 a) I can't believe Riko is only sixteen!
      I can't believe Riko is only sixteen.
   b) Why do you think Raj wants to become a pilot?
   c) Kristyna's brother was born three years later.
      Kristyna's brother was born three years later?
   d) The waves were as high as a house!
      The waves were as high as a house.
   e) How many times have you been to Delhi?

5 It felt as though the whole world was shaking. I had never experienced anything like it. Whatever was happening? I looked down and thought I might faint with fear. The rock I was standing on was splitting in half!

COMMAS (page 31)

1 a) ✓
   b) ✗ Sheena started to walk more quickly. She didn't want to be late again.
   c) ✗ I blushed to the roots of my hair. Everyone was staring at me.
   d) ✓
   e) ✗ The jacket was made of red velvet. It had gold buttons.

2 a) If the door is locked, get a key from the caretaker.
   b) The plane was unable to take off because there was ice on the runway.
   c) Often, the things we find most difficult end up being the most rewarding.
   d) Whenever I go to Istanbul, I bring back some Turkish sweets.
   e) We were never allowed in my father's office when he was working.
   f) Despite having eaten earlier, Kerry still came for a pizza with us.

3 a) 'Good morning, Donna. It's a lovely day, isn't it?'
   b) Although it was morning, a layer of thick, dark cloud still blocked the Sun.
   c) We were lucky enough to spot elephants, giraffes and lions, which were resting under a tree.
   d) Despite our best efforts, the room was far from cosy.
   e) If you want to swim, make sure you bring a swimming costume, a towel and plenty of sun cream, won't you?

4 a) Mrs Evans, who suffered from arthritis, had great difficulty climbing the fence.
   b) Most of the hotels in the town cater for the luxury market.
   c) Many of the people who were at the conference had travelled from abroad to be there.
   d) The castle, which stood at the mouth of the river, looked smaller than Chuck had expected.

5 a) Leave the area immediately if you hear three short, sharp blasts of the horn.
   b) My friend, who is very generous, bought a card, flowers and chocolates for my birthday.
   c) The ancient stone pots contained coins, bracelets and rings.
   d) In addition, students can take part in archery and rock climbing.

6 We tiptoed nervously into the dark, dank room. Arjun, who was carrying the torch, went ahead. As he swung the beam around, we could see piles of books, broken furniture, paintings tilted at drunken angles and what looked like a heap of rusting machine parts in the corner.

   Although it was obvious that Mr Pankhurst hadn't been in the room for years, I somehow felt his presence still. In my head I could hear his voice, puzzled yet stern, asking us what we thought we were doing.

   'I don't like this, Arjun,' I whispered. 'It's creepy, isn't it?'

ANSWERS

BRACKETS AND DASHES (page 33)

1 a) The characters (except for Rob) are all in their thirties.
   b) You will be working with both Xena (have you met her?) and Finn.
   c) Have you seen Clara's house (the one in Manchester)?
   d) Lars has lost so much weight (over three stone!) just by cutting out sugar.
   e) She is a well-known singer in Egypt.

2 a) ✓
   b) ✓
   c) ✗
   d) ✗

3 (Lines indicate good hyphenation points.)
   a) in|for|ma|tion
   b) ✓
   c) as|so|nance
   d) ✓
   e) beau|ti|ful

4 a) I use a news app in order to get up-to-date information.
   b) (Not needed)
   c) (Not needed)
   d) We were unable to make any long-term plans.

APOSTROPHES (page 34)

1 a) The children's diet consisted mainly of potatoes.
   b) Ray's car was parked at the top of the hill, next to Gloria's.
   c) Have you seen all the photos on Hamza's Facebook page?
   d) Marco is playing drums in Laura and Kit's band now.
   e) Mrs Jones's dog attacked Roger's cat.

2 a) Julio's laptop
   b) the company's website
   c) James's coat
   d) (Sounds unnatural)
   e) Ellie and Brandon's cat

3 Farah was nervous. <u>She'd</u> never given a speech in public before and she <u>didn't</u> know whether <u>she'd</u> be able to keep her voice steady.

   '<u>Don't</u> worry,' her friend Robyn reassured her. '<u>It'll</u> be fine. Remember, <u>you're</u> the expert in this subject. <u>You've</u> done so much research for this talk. <u>It's</u> bound to be interesting.'

4 a) he'd
   b) can't
   c) they've
   d) you'll
   e) it's
   f) it'll

5 a) I'm not sure whose shoes these are, but they may be Paul's.
   b) The elephant's owners wash him every day.
   c) David's not allowed to go in his parents' room.
   d) You can have some of Sara's biscuits if you're hungry.
   e) They've already met each other's families.
   f) That bag is Elena's, not yours.

6 a) We've bought bunk beds for the twins' room.
   b) We could go to Michel's house if you'd like to.
   c) Both of Dawn and Joe's children were born in the '90s.
   d) Let's watch the women's football on TV tomorrow.
   e) You'd better give Craig's book back now.
   f) We'll see them later – they'll be at the party.

COLONS AND SEMICOLONS (page 36)

1 a) ✗
   b) ✓
   c) ✓
   d) ✗
   e) ✓
   f) ✗

2 a) Mr Harris was only interested in one thing: cricket.
   b) My mother loved the idea of living in the countryside; my father disagreed.
   c) The scenery was spectacular: snow-capped mountains towered above us. (; also possible)
   d) Welcome drinks: 7.30 p.m.
   e) Macbeth is drawn to further evil; after murdering Duncan he kills his guards. (: also possible)
   f) Train times are as follows: 10.13 for Exeter and 11.25 for Leeds.

3 a) Make sure you have the following items: a waterproof coat; thick socks and gloves; a torch.
   b) Activities included in the price are: arts and crafts; paintballing; abseiling; swimming.
   c) The following foods are available from the campsite shop: fruit and veg; fresh and frozen meat or fish; crisps and confectionery.
   d) There are three basic rules in this class: speak and listen with respect; use only English; keep all mobile phones in your bags.

EFFECTIVE SPEECH PUNCTUATION (page 37)

1 a) ✗
   b) ✗
   c) ✓
   d) ✓

2 a) 'Hi, Larry<u>!</u>' shouted Hal. '<u>H</u>ow are you?'
   b) 'I've never been to Africa<u>,</u>' Shania said<u>.</u> 'I'd love to go there.'
   c) 'You must not leave the room<u>,</u>' the examiner instructed<u>,</u> '<u>u</u>nless there is an emergency<u>.</u>'
   d) Iman whispered<u>,</u> 'I've got a secret to tell you<u>.</u>'

3 a) 'Are you hungry?' she asked.
  b) 'I'm a teacher,' he said.
  c) 'Can I come in?' he asked.
  d) 'I'm absolutely freezing!' she exclaimed.
  e) 'I'd like a sandwich,' he said.

4 a) 'Do you have a coat?' Rowena asked. 'It's cold outside.'
  b) 'He won twenty thousand pounds!' Grace shrieked. 'That's more than I earn in a year.'
  c) Baz said, 'I don't like jazz much, do you?'
  d) 'The bus is waiting,' said our guide. 'We are leaving in five minutes.'
  e) 'My boss,' David said, 'is not going to like this!'

5 The woman in red robes took us to the castle gate.

  'Be careful,' she said. 'The forest is a dangerous place.'

  'Are there bears?' asked Ryan in a small voice.

  'There aren't any bears,' she said, 'but there are snakes. They don't often bite people, but when they do, few survive.'

  I put an arm around Ryan's shoulder. He looked deathly pale.

  'Don't worry,' I said. 'We're going to be fine, I know we are.'

  The woman shrugged.

  'Let's hope so,' she said doubtfully.

TEST YOUR UNDERSTANDING (page 39)

It was the end of another long[,] boring day[.] Tara and her brother Josh had been sitting at the window for hours, waiting for the sound of their parents['] car coming up the long drive. Although they were only eight and six[,] the children were used to being left alone. After all, what other choice was there[?]

If their parents did[n't] go to the factory every day[,] there wouldn't be any money to buy food. The Grand Master[,] who controlled all their lives[,] saw to that. The children didn't like it but they were used to it. They weren't usually scared to be left alone. However[,] today was different. Today they were definitely scared.

'They should be home by now[,]' said Josh in a quavery voice[.] 'I don't like it[!].'

'I'm sure they won't be long[,]' Tara reassured him, but in reality she was far from certain.

They had never been this late before[. I]n her heart, she knew that something was wrong. Everything had been strange that morning. Even the bird[s,] who usually sang to greet the day[,] had been silent in the eerie, grey dawn.

PART FIVE: PARAGRAPHS AND ORGANISATION

USING PARAGRAPHS EFFECTIVELY (page 40)

1 a) A new character is introduced to the story.
  b) A different idea, topic or event is being described.
  c) There is a time shift in the action being described.
  d) The speaker in a dialogue has changed.
  e) A different character's thoughts or actions are being described.

2 She noticed that he was looking tired and somewhat dishevelled, his hair lank and unwashed and his skin faintly pallid. Without warning, he crouched down to retrieve something from the canvas bag that lay at his feet and then stood up, with an air of triumph.

  'This is for you, Naomi!' he announced, brandishing a crumpled letter.

  'For me? What?' she replied, seemingly baffled at this development.

  'Yes, you'll understand once you've read it. It'll all make sense – trust me.'

  He turned on his heel and walked away.

  'Antonio, wait! I need to speak to you. Don't go!'

  'Sorry, I'm due somewhere else now. You'll be fine – you'll see,' he replied, walking backwards to face her as he said it.

  Later that afternoon, in the privacy of her bedroom and with trembling hands, Naomi ripped open the envelope.

3 There is a great deal of concern over the amount of time that young people are spending on their screens, be it mobile phones, tablets or laptops. Admittedly, a cursory glance around a café or other public place will reveal a significant proportion of people under twenty-five consulting a screen. Similarly, most parents nowadays will testify that it is sometimes a battle to persuade their offspring to put down their mobile phone during mealtimes. However, this is certainly not the whole story. // Let us consider for a moment what those young people are doing with their screens. Some of them will be 'chatting' with friends. It may not be 'face time' conversation, but it is conversation nonetheless, with all the pleasures and benefits that brings. After all, anything that mitigates the loneliness of twenty-first century existence has some merit. // Others, meanwhile, will be consuming social media which, contrary to its popular image, is not dominated solely by pictures of kittens and puppies. Indeed, social media is the medium through which many young people learn about current affairs, and there is more and more evidence to suggest that they are learning a considerable amount. Certainly if public marches are a barometer of youthful political engagement, this would seem to be the case.

4 <u>Travel broadens the mind, it is said.</u> A cliché this may be but, like all clichés, there is an element of truth to it. Many teenagers entering adulthood will only have lived in one country, or even one area of a country. Accordingly, however positive their experience of life, it will inevitably be limited. Overseas travel introduces young people to other languages, cultures and ways of life. This has the effect of opening up the mind to other ways of being in a way that is stimulating and enriching. // <u>It benefits young people to be challenged.</u> Very often, young people have lived sheltered lives in families where parents have made their arrangements and dealt with their problems. Though perfectly natural, this parent-child dynamic does not always equip young adults to deal with the rigours of modern life. Travel pulls young people out of their comfort zone and forces them to develop basic life skills. Airports and railways stations must be negotiated, strangers approached for information, food purchased, and very often, all in a different language. This is hugely character-building. // <u>We learn to appreciate our homes.</u> Most of us have grown up in centrally heated houses, with an array of electrical appliances at our disposal. Overseas travel on a budget is not always comfortable. Indeed, it can be quite gruelling. Consequently, we often return with a heightened appreciation of our homes and neighbourhoods.

HOW TO USE CONNECTIVES (page 44)

1 a) linking a similar idea
b) generalising
c) showing something's purpose
d) presenting a different idea
e) giving a specific example
f) adding to an idea

2 a) By way of contrast
b) most notably
c) Moreover
d) For this reason
e) evidently
f) on the whole

3 a) As a leader, she is courageous, calm and analytical. Furthermore, she is able to inspire confidence.
b) Some regard her as too tolerant and caring while conversely, some see her as not compassionate enough.
c) Her critics say that she has failed in some key areas, specifically energy and the environment.
d) She is good at dealing with conflict and is therefore particularly able to lead in these troubled times.
e) She is very logical, but equally she often comes up with creative solutions.
f) Her serious nature can be a disadvantage – for example, some have criticised her humourless speeches.

4 a) in stark contrast
b) equally
c) indeed
d) in particular
e) as a result

5 a) A punitive tax could be put in place to penalise this harmful practice. <u>Alternatively</u>, we could provide tax incentives to businesses who do not pollute in this way.
b) Her background was very privileged, <u>whereas</u> his had been poor.
c) She found the task difficult and at times thankless. <u>Nevertheless</u>, she persevered and, in the end, succeeded.
d) The scheme was pointless. It was unlikely that it would succeed. <u>Besides</u>, it was too expensive.
e) The global population is increasing; <u>hence</u> the need for greater food supplies.

TEST YOUR UNDERSTANDING (page 46)

Dear Sir/Madam,

I was disappointed to read a review of city-centre cafés in your newspaper (11th March), which failed to feature a single vegetarian or vegan café <u>despite</u> the existence of several in the city centre. As a long-time vegetarian who has recently turned vegan, I am saddened by this omission and would like to share my thoughts with you.

<u>Firstly</u>, I would like to point out the sheer number of non meat-eaters in the city. Whether for ethical, environmental or health reasons, over five per cent of the population of this country now chooses not to eat meat. This represents a considerable number of people. <u>Moreover</u>, the figure is set to increase dramatically with the vegan movement now going mainstream. <u>With this in mind,</u> would it not make sense to include establishments that cater for this large group of people in your round-up of the city's cafés?

Ironically, your café round-up was featured on the same page as an article encouraging us all to practise 'green, urban living', quite rightly extolling the virtues of practices <u>such as </u>cycling, recycling, etc. As a newspaper, you are <u>evidently</u> very much in favour of environmental initiatives. Indeed, this is partly why I read your paper. <u>However</u>, in the same spread, you miss the opportunity to tell people about the cafes in the city where they can eat sustainably. (For anyone who is interested, Café Rainbow on Hill Street is one such establishment, The Pod (Lawrence Street) and Friends' Café (Montreal Road) are two others.)

<u>Finally</u>, I would like to draw to your attention the upcoming Vegan Fair at the City Community College, May 5th. I look forward to seeing coverage of this exciting event in your newspaper.

Yours faithfully,

Jo Lynch